Understanding
EATING
DISORDERS

Dr Bob Palmer

Published by Family Doctor Publications Limited
in association with the British Medical Association

IMPORTANT NOTICE

This book is intended not as a substitute for personal medical advice but as a supplement to that advice for the patient who wishes to understand more about his or her condition.

Before taking any form of treatment YOU SHOULD ALWAYS CONSULT YOUR MEDICAL PRACTITIONER.

In particular (without limit) you should note that advances in medical science occur rapidly and some of the information about drugs and treatment contained in this booklet may very soon be out of date.

Family Doctor Publications, PO Box 4664, Poole, Dorset BH15 1NN

Medical Editor: Dr Tony Smith
Consultant Editor: Jane Sugarman
Cover Artist: Dave Eastbury
Artist: Dave Eastbury
Design: MPG Design, Blandford Forum, Dorset
Printing: Nuffield Press, Abingdon, Oxon, using acid-free paper

ISBN: 1 898205 74 4

Contents

Introduction

When you hear the words 'eating disorder', it can bring to mind a number of contrasting thoughts. You may remember a newspaper story about a teenager who starved herself to death. There may have been pictures of someone looking like a walking skeleton. An eating disorder may then appear to be a mysterious condition that is striking down children and teenagers at the threshold of promising lives. On the other hand, talk of eating disorders may conjure up stories of glamorous celebrities who have admitted to suffering from anorexia nervosa or bulimia. Then the conditions may have been portrayed in the press as a slimming regime that went too far, or as a foolish fad of the rich and famous, who are obsessed with their appearance.

You may not know what to think.

In fact, neither of these two examples gives a true picture of eating disorders. In this country there are tens of thousands of people who have these disorders. Most are not famous or glamorous. A very few may die from the conditions but very many will feel stuck and trapped by them. Eating disorders are real illnesses. They lead to real misery and suffering. They deserve to be taken seriously.

The possibility or the reality of an eating disorder is something that may well arise for anyone, either in themselves or in someone close to them. So if you suspect that someone you care about might have an eating disorder, what should you do and how can you best help? Should you be out of your mind with worry if your daughter goes on a diet? Should you tell a friend not to be silly when she says that she is feeling fat and unattractive? Could making too much fuss make matters worse? And what if you find yourself getting overly concerned about

your weight and preoccupied with food?

This book aims to describe and explain eating disorders. It will discuss the causes and effects of these conditions. Hopefully, it will help you take a better informed and more sensible view should questions like these arise for you. I have said that eating disorders should be taken seriously but they are not a reason for panic. Effective treatment is available. Help can be obtained from family doctors, from specialist hospital clinics and from eating disorder organisations and self-help groups. Most of those who have an eating disorder recover safely, with or without treatment, even though they may have spent months and years battling with their condition.

KEY POINTS

✓ Many people suffer from eating disorders

✓ Eating disorders are rarely fatal illnesses

✓ Eating disorders can cause real misery and suffering

✓ Most people who have an eating disorder recover safely

What are eating disorders?

The term 'eating disorder' is usually applied to two conditions. These are anorexia nervosa and bulimia nervosa. They are closely related and indeed there is even some debate as to whether they are best thought of as different manifestations of one basic disorder.

ANOREXIA NERVOSA

Anorexia nervosa literally means 'loss of appetite for nervous reasons'. It is characterised by weight loss. However, a woman with anorexia nervosa has not lost her appetite. She has lost weight because she is suppressing her urge to eat.

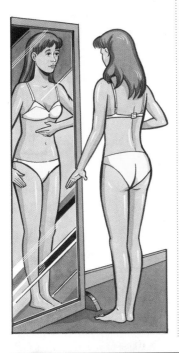

This eating restraint is often due to her ideas about body weight and fears about getting fat. She will often experience herself as being fat even when she is very thin. This is referred to as having a distorted body image.

The majority of people who develop anorexia nervosa do so in their teens or early twenties.

BULIMIA NERVOSA

Bulimia nervosa is diagnosed chiefly by the presence of binge eating. However, bingeing in bulimia nervosa is not simply an occasional splurge or indulgence. It involves eating an unusually large quantity of food, often in a rather frantic manner, and is accompanied

DIAGNOSTIC CRITERIA FOR ANOREXIA

- There is weight loss leading to a body weight of at least 15 per cent below the normal or expected weight for height or age. In children, this could be due to lack of weight gain rather than weight loss.

- The weight loss is self-induced by avoiding fattening foods.

- There is a self-perception of being too fat, with an overwhelming dread of fatness. This leads to a self-imposed low weight threshold.

- There is a widespread hormonal disorder which may lead to amenorrhoea (lack of menstruation) in women and a loss of sexual interest and potency in men.

by a sense that the eating is out of control.

People with bulimia nervosa also have an exaggerated fear of being fat. But unlike sufferers of anorexia, their body weight may be high, low or average. They often try to restrain their eating but the balance between restraint and bingeing may produce a kind of stability of body weight, albeit a precarious one. Furthermore, binge eating is often followed by self-induced vomiting or laxative abuse, again because the sufferer hopes to avoid gaining weight.

Bulimia nervosa tends to begin at a slightly higher age than anorexia nervosa, typically in women in their late teens and twenties. It is thought to be more common than anorexia nervosa.

It is possible to have a mixture of the features of anorexia nervosa and bulimia nervosa. The person may then be said to have bulimic anorexia nervosa. It is also possible to have some, but not all, of the features of one of the conditions. The usual terms then are 'atypical anorexia' or 'atypical bulimia', although sometimes the term 'partial syndrome' is used. Such atypical and partial states may actually be more common than the full disorders.

ARE THERE OTHER EATING DISORDERS?

Two other conditions are sometimes

DIAGNOSTIC CRITERIA FOR BULIMIA

- There are recurrent episodes of overeating at least twice a week over a period of three months. Large amounts of food are consumed in short periods of time.

- There is a persistent preoccupation with eating, and a strong desire or sense of compulsion to eat.

- The person attempts to counteract the fattening effects of food by one or more of the following: self-induced vomiting, self-induced purging, alternating periods of starvation, drugs such as appetite suppressants or diuretics.

- There is a self-perception of being too fat, with an excessive fear of fatness.

described as eating disorders but are not usually included as such in medical classifications.

Obesity

One is obesity, which can be a serious problem but is not always associated with disordered or unusual eating. So although some obese people may have an eating disorder and have some of the characteristics of bulimia, obesity itself is not considered an eating disorder.

Compulsive eating

The other condition, often referred to as compulsive eating, is a vague term that has not been clearly defined. It often seems to apply to some eating patterns within bulimia nervosa or a partial syndrome.

CASE HISTORY

Heather: a story of anorexia

Heather was the younger daughter of two schoolteachers. Her early childhood was settled and happy, but things started to go wrong when she was about 14 and her sister Fiona was 16. Their father, who was then 46, had a heart attack. He had to stop working and abandon his chance of becoming a headmaster, which had been his ambition. He came to be prone to bouts of depression. He was touchy and irritable, especially with Fiona.

Over the next two years, rows between the two of them dominated the household.

Much to her parents' disapproval, Fiona left school and got a job in a local record shop. At 18 she became pregnant and left home to live with her boyfriend. Her father was devastated, and said that he would have nothing more to do with Fiona. Her mother and Heather continued to visit her secretly.

When Fiona's baby was born there was some reconciliation, but her father continued to be low. He often complained of chest pain and sometimes said that Fiona had ruined his life. Heather's mother struggled to hold things together, working hard at her job, acting as a go between and looking after her sick and troubled husband.

Heather, on the other hand, was doing well in school. Her parents were delighted when her teachers suggested she try for a place at Oxford or Cambridge. She was studying modern languages, her father's subject, and he coached her in the evenings. He described himself as her 'trainer' and talked of Oxbridge entrance as 'the Olympics'. He also encouraged her to go jogging, making pronouncements about a healthy mind in a healthy body. As his disappointment with Fiona developed so did his involvement with his younger daughter. Heather valued his interest but she was increasingly aware of the extent of his expectation. She began to fear letting him down.

Heather started going out with a boy named Andrew. She soon became aware of a sense of conflict between her wish to spend time with Andrew and her wish to devote herself to her studies. She also felt that her father disapproved of her boyfriend and that he feared that she would 'end up like Fiona'.

One weekend she stayed out late, worrying her parents. Her father had an angina attack and her mother reminded Heather how important it was for her father not to be upset. She began to make excuses to Andrew and before long he left her for another girl. Heather felt heartbroken and secretly angry that her father seemed so pleased at the end of the relationship.

She felt confused and uncertain, but vowed to pull herself together. She decided to try for Oxford and dreamed about being a success there. She could wait for her reward. In the meantime she would work hard, save money, get fit and even lose some weight as she had been promising herself she would do for months.

At first, everything went well. Heather worked hard. Her father was pleased. Her mother seemed more relaxed. Even Fiona began to visit more often. Heather produced

a timetable for her studies and her father helped to plan it all out. She lost a few pounds by taking up running and following what her mother called a 'sensible diet'.

Heather felt good much of the time, but sometimes when studying her mind would wander. She would then chide herself for wasting time daydreaming. She worried about what would happen if she didn't do well. She felt bad when one evening she realised she had eaten an entire packet of biscuits. She weighed herself and discovered she had put back on three pounds. She felt that things were slipping. Somehow she must get things back on track.

She produced a new timetable which covered all of her activities, including running, eating and studying. She rationed the times when she would allow herself to get a cup of coffee and just one biscuit. Soon she stopped the biscuits altogether.

As the weeks went by, Heather lost more weight. At 16 she had weighed about nine stones (58 kg). A year later, she weighed just six and a half stones (42 kg) and her periods had stopped. She was now preoccupied with just two things – succeeding at her studies and controlling her weight. She feared that she would fail at both.

She was studying so much that even her father advised her to ease off. Her mother was worried about her eating but Heather would lie, telling her she had eaten earlier in the day. She wore baggy clothes and avoided letting her mother see her undressed. She often felt fat but knew she looked thin. She thought about food a lot but distracted herself with still more studying. Once she got up in the middle of the night and ate two packets of biscuits and a large tub of ice cream. She then tried to make herself vomit but could not manage it. This reinforced her feeling that if she allowed herself to eat freely, everything would get out of control.

> *'Just two things seemed important: her studies and controlling her weight'*

That autumn, Heather was rejected by Oxford. By now it was evident that she was very thin. At Christmas, her behaviour led to major upsets and rows in the family. Finally, early in the New Year, her parents persuaded her to see the family doctor. When weighed at the surgery, she was just under six stones (37 kg). It was clear now that she was suffering from anorexia nervosa.

CASE HISTORY

Susan: a story of bulimia

Susan was the elder child and only daughter of a policeman and a nurse. When she was eleven her father left home and went to live with another woman. Susan was very angry, and had almost no contact with her father for the next eight years. She tried to be supportive to her mother. They became very close. Her mother tended to confide in her to an unusual degree and together they looked after Susan's brother, Sean, who had been only six when his father left.

Susan had no major regrets when her parents were finally divorced two years later. However, she was not sure how she felt when her mother started going out with John, a colleague from work, and within six months announced that they were to marry. Susan was just 15 when her mother married John and he moved in. She told herself that she was pleased for her mother, but she missed their closeness.

She felt uncomfortable with John. He tried hard to be friendly but tended to tease her about her going out on dates, her taste in clothes and about her worry about her appearance. He also teased her about the way in which she was always going on diets which lasted just a day or two.

Over the next year Susan felt more and more isolated and unhappy at home. She tried to spend as little time there as possible. She went out almost every evening, often ending up drinking a lot. This added to her difficulties. She greatly resented it when John started to behave like a strict father. There were lots of rows between them. Later that year, she took her GCSE exams but the results were disappointing. She was unsure what to do but signed up for a course at the local college.

When Susan was 17 she met a professional footballer called Mark, who was seven years her senior. It was a difficult relationship, because although Mark was lively and glamorous he also seemed to be rather unreliable. Just before Christmas, as she was wondering whether to finish with him, she found that she was pregnant. To her surprise Mark seemed pleased at the prospect of being a father, and they decided to live together. Her mother and stepfather protested but Susan suspected that they were relieved that she was leaving home.

She dropped out of her course at Easter and gave birth to a baby boy, Rory, in July. She had put on a lot of weight during her pregnancy and afterwards felt fat and unattractive. She wanted to lose weight but found it difficult. Sometimes she was uninterested in food, while at other times she ate far more than she intended. She became mildly depressed and miserable.

She loved Rory but found motherhood overwhelming. With the start of the football season, Mark was often away and seemed less interested in the baby now. As the months went by the couple fought more and more. Susan worried that Mark would meet other women on his trips away from home. And he became possessive, hating her to go out even with her old girlfriends. She felt increasingly unhappy and isolated, much as she had done a year or so before.

This time, however, she felt that there was no obvious escape route. She certainly did not want to go back to her mother's house. She also regretted giving up her education, but when she talked to Mark about going back to college he accused her of wanting to meet other men. In the midst of a row, he called her fat, ugly and boring. He said that she had 'let herself go'. Susan was angry and upset, but secretly these were the very things she had been thinking about herself.

She made another resolution to lose weight. She started by going on a crash diet. She was pleased to lose some weight quickly but felt unhappy, hungry, preoccupied with food and irritable. One evening Mark telephoned yet again to say that he would not be home. She felt angry, upset and out of control. She stuffed herself with food until she could physically eat no more. Then she felt panicky and guilty. She made herself vomit. The next day she resolved to eat even less, but a week later she binged again. Much as she tried to stop, she felt caught in a pattern and soon was bingeing several times a week. Although her eating was now wildly erratic her weight stayed much the same.

Susan left Mark shortly after Rory's first birthday. The final straw came when Mark hit her in an outburst of jealousy. She had recently re-established contact with her father and he threatened to 'sort out' Mark if she stayed. At first she went home to her mother. After a few weeks she moved to a flat on her own and started to build a new life.

In some ways, things began to look up. However, she still felt lonely and unsure of herself. At times she would feel quite desperate and even thought of trying to kill herself. She resumed some contact with Mark but just as friends. She went out occasionally with her old friends and attended a regular aerobics class. She started a course at the local college and talked of eventually going on to

SUSAN'S FATHER LEFT HOME WHEN SHE WAS ELEVEN...

DON'T WORRY MUM, I'LL LOOK AFTER YOU!

HER MOTHER RE-MARRIED WHEN SUSAN WAS 15...

YOU'RE NOT ON ANOTHER *DIET* ARE YOU?

AT 17 SUSAN HAD A BABY BOY WITH MARK, HER BOYFRIEND!

THE RELATIONSHIP GREW MORE DIFFICULT AND TENSE...

YOU'RE *FAT* AND *BORING*, YOU'VE LET YOURSELF GO!

HOW *DARE* YOU!

university. To other people it looked as if all was well, but secretly her life revolved around a battle with bingeing and vomiting. She had become stuck within bulimia nervosa.

KEY POINTS

✓ The two recognised eating disorders are anorexia and bulimia nervosa

✓ Anorexia nervosa is characterised by excessive weight loss due to restricting eating

✓ The main feature of bulimia nervosa is binge eating – eating large quantities of food often in a frantic way with a feeling of loss of control

✓ Both eating disorders seem to arise through self-imposed eating restraint often motivated by concern about body weight and shape

✓ It is possible to have some but not all of the features of the disorders or a mixture of the two

Some features of eating disorders

Some of the features of the eating disorders, such as weight loss, are visible and obvious. Others are psychological and impossible to see. As the two conditions are so intertwined, people with either anorexia or bulimia will often exhibit many of the same signs and symptoms. A number of these focus on food and its consumption and on ideas about weight and shape.

CHANGES IN BODY WEIGHT

Loss of weight is a primary symptom of anorexia nervosa. If the weight loss is extreme it can be a real threat to health. Of course, height must be taken into account in assessing weight loss as must the

SIGNS AND SYMPTOMS OF AN EATING DISORDER

- Changes in body weight
- Eating restraint
- Binge eating
- Fear of losing control
- Disturbed body image
- Vomiting
- Laxative abuse
- Excessive exercising
- Amenorrhoea and hormonal changes
- Psychological features

weight before the illness started. There is some evidence that every person has a weight or weight range where their body tends to settle naturally. This weight may not be the so-called 'ideal' weight found in weight tables or the weight that the person might prefer to be, given an entirely free choice. As a general rule of thumb, a weight loss of 10 to 15 per cent for someone of average body weight is significant. A loss of 25 to 30 per cent is even more cause for concern because it may of itself threaten health and well-being. Anorexia nervosa occurring in a child who has not finished growing can be especially damaging. The child may end up with stunted growth if the disorder is long lasting.

People with bulimia nervosa may have a weight that is stable. However, the stability is fragile as it reflects a tenuous balance of binge eating, attempted restraint and the person's attempt to eliminate extra calories, for example, by vomiting or using laxatives, or taking excessive exercise. She may also have wide fluctuations in weight.

EATING RESTRAINT

In the stories of Heather and Susan, both of them were concerned about their body weight and both of them

attempted to slim by cutting down on the amount of food eaten or avoiding 'fattening' foods. This is what is called eating restraint. In our society the most common reason given for eating restraint is the wish to lose weight. However, it can also be undertaken for other reasons, for instance because of a desire for self-punishment, for self-purification or other reasons connected with ideas of health or religion. Some cases of so-called atypical eating disorders seem to arise through eating restraint motivated in these more unusual ways.

Eating restraint has serious consequences. The young woman who restrains her eating while still retaining a normal appetite will tend to become hungry, pre-occupied with food, impulsive with regard to food, and more emotional

and irritable than usual. Someone who has anorexia nervosa, in particular, may feel all of these things, although sometimes it may be difficult to admit them even to herself. They are the predictable consequences of semi-starvation.

The eating patterns of people with eating disorders vary widely. In general, those with anorexia nervosa will eat small amounts of a narrow range of foods that they consider 'safe' or less 'fattening'. Sometimes eating becomes a form of ritual that has to be done in a certain way and at a certain time. Other people, particularly close family members, may become involved in these rituals. They may feel that going along with them is the only way to get the sufferer to eat at all.

Strangely, some people with

anorexia like to spend time cooking and preparing food for others. This may be a way of coping with their preoccupation with food and at the same time demonstrating to themselves and others their own self-control.

Apart from bingeing, people with bulimia nervosa may appear to have more normal eating habits. Some may eat very little except during a binge, but most will appear to eat normally or seem to be dieting in a fairly commonplace manner. Their problem and its associated suffering are easier to keep secret than is anorexia nervosa.

BINGE EATING

Binge eating is the central feature of bulimia nervosa. It may also occur in anorexia nervosa. A typical binge involves the consumption of large amounts of food in a short period of time with an accompanying sense of loss of control. At worst, the person feels frantically driven by some inner force to eat, and to eat in a way that is frightening, upsetting or even painful. It is quite different to the pleasurable overindulgence

common on occasions like Christmas, which may also sometimes be described as a binge.

Binge eating is probably triggered by various factors including emotional turmoil. However, it is likely that the most important is an on-going attempt to restrain eating. If someone is in a semi-starved state, the drive to eat is likely to be increased. It makes sense for human beings to have a built-in mechanism which leads to food preoccupation when food is scarce and an increased drive to eat when food is found. When the deprivation is self-imposed, the sufferers may feel guilty if they give up and eat. It may come to feel like a major defeat or a moral collapse. On the other hand, it may feel like a drug trip or a drunken splurge. The emotions experienced during a binge vary from one person to another, but a sense of being out of control is a crucial part of bingeing. Afterwards the person often feels upset and even disgusted with herself. A frequent reaction is to resolve to control her eating and eat even less in future, ignoring the fact that this very resolve makes further bingeing more likely.

FEAR OF LOSING CONTROL

The fear of being out of control is central to much of the thinking of people with eating disorders.

The person with anorexia nervosa may be frightened of bingeing but fears gaining weight even more. She feels that unless she is vigilant and takes steps to avoid it, her weight will rise uncontrollably. Even the smallest rise in weight is frightening, whereas losing weight is reassuring. By responding to this fear she continues to control her eating and inevitably the weight goes down.

A person with bulimia nervosa may share something of this fear, although bingeing makes weight loss less predictable. However, for neither sufferer is there much sense of having an 'automatic pilot' which will control weight and eating habits. The entire business of weight and eating control feels unstable and unsafe.

Sometimes fears of loss of control can become so extreme that an individual feels that any lapse will lead to everything going wrong. For instance, someone with anorexia nervosa may believe that eating just a small amount of what she considers a 'fattening' food will cause her to become obese. Any rational objection to such a view is pushed aside because that is how it feels to the sufferer. People with eating disorders, especially anorexia nervosa, usually experience their bodies subjectively. They see themselves as being quite different from how they appear to those around them.

DISTURBED BODY IMAGE

Most people with eating disorders see their bodies as objects of concern and worry. Many are described as having a disturbance of their body image. This is sometimes illustrated by a picture of an emaciated young woman looking into a mirror and seeing a reflection of someone who is grossly overweight. Such extreme distortion is not always found even in those with the most severe anorexia nervosa, although lesser degrees of disturbance are common in those with eating disorders. Moreover,

such a picture oversimplifies a complex issue.

All of us, to some degree, experience our bodies in a way that reflects our beliefs and our wider view of ourselves. Other people who are concerned with their body size, such as genuinely obese people and pregnant women, share with those with eating disorders a tendency to misjudge body size and shape.

The problem for most eating disorder sufferers is not so much that they see themselves as fat. Instead, they cannot easily dismiss the feeling that they are fat or at risk of becoming fat if they fail to keep things in control. Such feelings are usually quite independent of their actual weight. So someone may acknowledge that they feel just as fat at six stones (38 kg) as they did at 10 stones (63 kg). They know that this does not make sense but cannot rid themselves of the feeling.

ABNORMAL METHODS OF WEIGHT CONTROL

Eating restraint is the most commonly adopted method of attempting to control weight. But people with both of the eating disorders may try additional ways to avoid weight gain, especially if they have succumbed to binge eating. The most common methods are self-induced vomiting and the abuse of laxatives and diuretics. Some people chew food and then spit it

Then the person may be in real danger. For instance, the sufferer may experience seizures or the heart may be affected or even stop, although fortunately this is rare.

However, erosion of tooth enamel and damage to the tissues of the mouth, throat or gullet are much more common complications of repeated vomiting. It can also lead to swelling of the parotid salivary glands, which may give the person a 'hamster cheek' appearance.

Another method is the excessive use of laxatives. The abuse of laxatives is based upon the idea that if the passage of food through the gut is speeded up, the amount that is absorbed will be cut down. This is not true, but still some people take enormous quantities of laxatives to try to achieve this effect. In doing so they are taking the same sort of risks with their health as those who vomit. This is because the main effect of taking laxatives is to stop the reabsorption of fluid and salts from the gut. Excessive use can cause severe depletion of vital fluids and salts. Although the body weight may change markedly after a big dose of laxatives, this reflects only a change in the amount of fluid in the body. There is no change in body substance or fat. And when water or fluids are taken in again, the body weight will increase.

The same is true of the abuse of diuretics, or water tablets. Doctors

out without swallowing as an alternative to vomiting.

Vomiting shortly after eating is obviously an effective way of reducing the amount of food absorbed by the body. Vomiting is usually brought on by stimulating the back of the throat with something such as the finger or a toothbrush. However, vomiting is dangerous. Repeated vomiting tends to deplete the body of the salts and ions, especially potassium, which must be kept in balance for the body to work properly. The body works hard to keep things in balance but it can be overwhelmed.

prescribe powerful diuretics for a variety of reasons including the treatment of heart failure. However, mild diuretics can be bought over the counter and when taken in high doses can have damaging effects. Abusing laxatives or diuretics can lead to the body's fluid balance becoming so out of kilter that fluid retention, weight gain and swelling (oedema) occur.

EXCESSIVE EXERCISING

People with eating disorders will often take excessive amounts of exercise in an attempt to control weight. Again, the effect of exercise on weight loss is often exaggerated. It is in truth rather small. There is no doubt that, in general, exercise has real advantages in promoting fitness and health. However, people with eating disorders often drive themselves into frantic activity because they believe that it will help them avoid weight gain.

Usually they will exercise alone. They may attend several aerobic classes each week or even every day, go jogging and also exercise at home. The whole process may become so much a part of their emotionally charged routine that any thought of stopping becomes frightening. Only by going on and on and on can the fantasies of loss of control be kept in check. Any positive benefit of exercise is outweighed by the emotional and physical costs of pushing a body weakened by weight loss or metabolic imbalance into a programme that is quite literally punishing.

AMENORRHOEA AND HORMONAL CHANGES

Amenorrhoea is the medical term for an absence of menstrual periods, and it is one of the key features of anorexia nervosa. This is because anorexia nervosa leads to important changes in the hormones, the body's natural chemical messengers that help to regulate the meta-bolism and the reproductive functions of the body.

Similar changes occur in sufferers from bulimia nervosa even when they maintain an average weight, but these changes are less profound and consistent. This is probably because the changes in anorexia nervosa are largely caused by the loss of body weight itself.

In growing children, the normal increase in body weight and body fat seems to play a part in promoting the physical changes of puberty. Hormonal changes are triggered as the body weight passes a certain threshold. These changes eventually result in menstruation in girls and parallel, although less evident, developments in boys. Their bodies could be described as being 'switched on' by physical growth.

With weight loss this process seems to go into reverse. The body 'switches off' the hormonal systems that sustain menstruation and the periods stop. If the girl has yet to start her periods their onset will be delayed.

This switching off may represent a built-in protection against pregnancy in times of food scarcity and starvation. But when the food deprivation is self-imposed for emotional reasons, the effects of the hormonal changes can take on many meanings. For instance, the girl may feel less sexual or less grown up. If she has been struggling with the emotional upheaval of adolescence, this may come as a relief. For others, the chief experience is of a loss of sexual feeling and libido. For most sufferers, these types of changes just add to the sense that life has become changed, confused, unpredictable and frightening.

Amenorrhoea is the outward sign of hormonal changes which indicate that the whole reproductive system is closed down. Women with amenorrhoea caused by anorexia nervosa are almost always unable to conceive because they are not ovulating.

The thinning of bones, known as osteoporosis, is another important consequence of anorexia nervosa. This can lead to fragility and fractures. It is probably caused by the hormonal changes, although poor nutrition may play a part.

Other hormones, such as thyroid and growth hormone, are also changed by the weight loss of anorexia nervosa but the effects are less evident and probably less important.

OTHER PHYSICAL COMPLICATIONS

There are many other physical complications of eating disorders but most are rare. Furthermore, they tend to occur only in the most severe cases. However, there is a wide range of minor physical symptoms that are not specific but nevertheless are often found in people with eating disorders. These include symptoms such as bloating, constipation, wind, weakness and fainting. Self-starvation and bingeing are just not good for the body and it is likely to complain and answer back.

PSYCHOLOGICAL FEATURES

Many of the features already described, such as body image disturbance and worries about loss of control, are psychological rather than physical. But there are others which are less specific but still important. Most, if not all, people with anorexia nervosa and bulimia nervosa are unhappy and troubled. In particular, they usually have low self-esteem and a deep-seated lack of confidence.

Many people with eating disorders are anxious and depressed. Others have noticeable symptoms of an obsessive disorder, such as checking rituals. Some people with eating disorders use additional, potentially damaging, ways of coping with difficult emotions. For instance, they may abuse alcohol or drugs. Some will go through crises in which they will feel suicidal or experience the impulse to damage themselves. Many will find that their relationships with others are changed by the effects of their illness.

KEY POINTS

✓ Weight loss always occurs with anorexia nervosa but not necessarily with bulimia nervosa

✓ Sufferers often see certain foods as 'good' or 'bad'. They feel that some foods are more likely to cause them to become fat, or lead to a binge

✓ Most anorexia nervosa sufferers have a disturbed body image. They may feel that they are overweight, even when they are not

✓ Purging by vomiting or taking laxatives is common after bingeing

✓ Women with anorexia nervosa usually stop menstruating

Who is affected?

Almost anyone can develop an eating disorder. However, not all types of people are at equal risk of doing so. The most striking fact is that women develop eating disorders much more frequently than men. Only one in ten or fewer of people presenting for help with an eating disorder is male. However, the balance between boys and girls is less skewed in the youngest sufferers, that is, those who are in their early teens or even younger.

WHEN DO EATING DISORDERS OCCUR?

Eating disorders usually occur in young people. Although anorexia nervosa may begin as young as ten or occur for the first time in women in their thirties or later, the peak age for developing the disorder is in the mid to late teens. Bulimia nervosa tends to occur a little later, typically in the late teens and twenties, and is rare in those below fifteen. The age at which young women are at the greatest risk probably coincides with the age when the greatest proportion of women are uncomfortable or dissatisfied with their bodies. For girls, the physical changes involved in growing into adult women are greater, or at least more evident, than for men. Furthermore, these changes often seem to have greater personal and social meaning. Weight concern and slimming behaviour are common at these times.

WHO IS MOST AT RISK?

It may well be that the risk of developing an eating disorder is increased by any kind of slimming.

So it is hardly surprising that young women such as dancers, athletes and models, who are especially concerned about body weight and shape and who are especially likely to engage in slimming, are also at greater risk of developing an eating disorder. Of course, for every person who attempts to slim and then goes on to develop anorexia nervosa or bulimia nervosa, there are many more who set out to slim in a similar way but remain well. Later there will be discussion about what may tip the balance toward an individual developing an eating

disorder. Nevertheless, if there are more people slimming there are likely to be more people who fall ill with eating disorders, just as the more people there are who drink alcohol the more people there will be who become problem drinkers. Far fewer men than women attempt to slim. The difference in rates of slimming behaviour is unlikely to be the sole explanation for the greater risk in young women, but it seems likely that it is an important reason.

In the past it was thought that most people who had eating disorders came from the better-off sections of society. Anorexia nervosa in particular was thought of as largely a problem of the so-called middle and upper classes. If this was ever truly the case, it is no longer so. Certainly, no social group is immune.

Other myths that go around are that most sufferers from anorexia nervosa are especially intelligent and especially 'good', as children, and that those with bulimia nervosa are striving upwardly mobile types who live life in the fast lane. These caricatures seem to be quite unjustified even as generalisations. Of course some people who develop eating disorders do broadly resemble these stereotypes but most do not. They are unhelpful.

MEN AND EATING DISORDERS

As was stated above only a small minority of people presenting for the treatment of eating disorders are male. There is almost certainly a large difference in rates of occurrence of the disorders between the two sexes. Bulimia nervosa seems especially rare in men.

Some people suggest that eating disorders may be becoming more common in men. The symptoms experienced by men are closely similar to those of women. Even the hormonal changes are more or less the same. However, it is possible that more men and boys go unrecognised and undiagnosed because eating disorders are often wrongly thought to afflict only women. In men, the reasons behind the development of an eating disorder, that is, the ideas that link eating restraint with wider personal issues, may involve the desire to be slim. They may, however, include ideas about fitness, health or quasi-religious fasting more often than in women.

HOW MANY PEOPLE HAVE EATING DISORDERS?

It is difficult to be sure how many people suffer from eating disorders. In the United Kingdom at present, the best estimates suggest that about one young woman in a hundred has bulimia nervosa and probably somewhat fewer have anorexia nervosa. But of course not all sufferers are young women. So in total perhaps two or three people per thousand have a diagnosable eating disorder. A further two or three people are likely to have atypical or partial syndromes. (Such people have some but not all of the symptoms of the typical eating disorders. Nevertheless they may have very significant problems.) This means that in this country there are tens of thousands of people whose lives revolve painfully around weight and eating and their control. Any group practice of family doctors is likely to have a dozen or so people with eating disorders on their list.

The number of people with eating disorders probably varies from country to country and from time to time. It is necessary to say 'probably' because there is only rather poor information about the rates of eating disorders in people in the past or today in many countries. However, there is some evidence that eating disorders are more common than they were 30 or 40 years ago. Indeed, bulimia nervosa was recognised and described as a distinct disorder only in the late 1970s. The numbers of women presenting with bulimia nervosa has risen steadily since that time. Now in most clinics they outnumber sufferers from anorexia nervosa. However, it is almost certain that for every one sufferer who presents for assessment and treatment there is at least one other who does not. Many people do not seek or do not successfully find professional help for their problem.

KEY POINTS

✓ Women are affected much more often than men

✓ Eating disorders usually but not always begin with slimming

✓ Eating disorders commonly begin in the teens and early twenties

✓ Body-conscious women, such as models and dancers, are particularly vulnerable

✓ Eating disorders have probably become more common over recent decades

Why do people develop eating disorders?

The question of why people develop eating disorders is a difficult one to answer. It may be that there is no one answer, or too many answers. There are many factors that appear to trigger the development of eating disorders. We are fairly confident about the role of some, but the importance of others is still unclear.

There are certainly plenty of theories about the influences that are thought to be important in causing anorexia or bulimia nervosa. Some people are convinced that certain kinds of family problems or childhood traumas could be a cause. Others blame the media or the pervasive influence of the fashion industry.

Still others may emphasise anything from sexual politics to zinc deficiency.

Whenever you find lots of competing theories about something, it is a fair bet that no one has really got to the bottom of the problem. In that sense, there is perhaps no answer to the question of what causes eating disorders. In another sense, there may be as many answers to the question as there are sufferers. In very general terms, eating disorders seem to be linked with and may be triggered by unhappiness and emotional difficulty. The roots of such unhappiness are specific and personal. No two people are exactly alike. So any statements about the

> **'Eating disorders seem to be triggered by unhappiness and emotional difficulty'**

causes of eating disorders will be generalisations. Nevertheless, generalisations can be useful as a guide. The following possible causes are considered important when trying to understand why eating disorders occur.

THE FEAR OF FATNESS AND THE DESIRE TO BE SLIM

Eating restraint is a part of almost all eating disorders. The most common reason for restraining eating is to try to lose weight. The whole situation may become complicated, but many people who end up with an eating disorder seem to start off simply trying to slim.

Of course, the reason why someone decides to start slimming in the first place may already be complex. By definition someone who sets out to lose weight is dissatisfied with herself or, at the very least, with some aspect of her body. Often the dissatisfaction may be more than just unhappiness with her shape and appearance. It may become focused on the body because the slimmer feels that weight and shape are both of great importance and relatively easily

controlled and changed. These are widely held ideas.

SOCIAL PRESSURES

Within our culture being slim is associated with being attractive, healthy and successful. This is especially true for women. Plumpness, although prized in the past, is now disparaged.

Furthermore, there is a major industry which claims to provide all the advice and the means that the slimmer needs to achieve a new figure and through that a new self-confidence. The slimming industry is closely linked with fashion, advertising and the media. All together they exert a powerful influence on women, especially young women. But this is a general influence. Taken on its own, it cannot explain why some women develop eating disorders but most do not. Furthermore, it may be argued that the media reflect the wider culture as much as they promote it. It is the familiar problem of the chicken and the egg.

FAMILY INFLUENCES

It seems to be the case that both anorexia and bulimia nervosa tend to run in families. Recent research suggests that susceptibility to eating disorders can be inherited. The evidence for genetic transmission is stronger in the case of anorexia nervosa than it is for bulimia nervosa. However, it is certainly true that most children learn much of their eating behaviour and attitudes from their parents. The family is likely to be important in both of these ways.

There is also much theorising

about the possible role of other kinds of family influences. For instance, it has been suggested that anorexia nervosa sufferers come from families who are very close emotionally, but where it is difficult for them to develop a sense of their own individuality and independence. Again, it is difficult to be sure whether particular ways of relating are causing the problem or are caused by it, or a bit of both. 'Normal' families vary a great deal. Furthermore, it is difficult to be sure what should be the 'normal' reaction of a family to the apparently wilful self-starvation of one of its members.

> ‘No one type of person gets eating disorders’

This having been said, it would be surprising if such family factors did not have some influence on the development of eating disorders. However, it is not yet clear whether particular styles of family interaction increase the risk of a person developing an eating disorder. Certainly no one pattern applies to all sufferers.

CHILDHOOD TRAUMAS

Another idea which has been widely considered is the role of bad experiences in childhood, particularly sexual abuse. Until fairly recently, the whole issue of childhood sexual abuse was largely neglected. This is no longer so. It is now clear that a substantial minority of children have been sexually exploited by adults. It is also clear that such abuse can have lasting effects upon that child as she or he grows up. These effects are likely to include an increased vulnerability to psychiatric illness in general. Around a third of women with eating disorders report some sexually abusive experience, and this may have played some part in the development of their disorder. However, women with other kinds of emotional illness report at least as many such experiences.

Thus there is unlikely to be any specific link between eating disorders and sexual abuse, over and above the general effect of such abuse making those so abused more vulnerable to psychiatric illness. But people who develop eating disorders have probably had more than their fair share of troubles of all kinds in their childhood. This may be especially so for those suffering from bulimia nervosa.

LOW SELF-ESTEEM

It is difficult to define any one type of young woman who is especially likely to develop an eating disorder.

However, two features do seem to be characteristic of many sufferers.

First, most have low self-esteem. They have real doubts about their own worth and competence. These doubts are often kept hidden and may be dealt with in all sorts of ways, from social retreat to exhibitionist bravado. Nevertheless, whatever appears to be the case on the outside, inside the sufferer feels very unsure of herself.

The second feature characteristic of many sufferers is that they find it difficult to deal openly with problematic emotions. They tend to try to keep the lid on difficult feelings. This may have something to do with their personality, for instance they may be obsessional and perfectionist.

It may also be something in their circumstances, such as a particular fear of upsetting or damaging other people. Either way, they are frightened that things will get out of control. Somehow these ideas about emotional control get mixed up with ideas about the control of weight and eating.

In general, eating disorders seem to arise in the midst of the

difficult business of growing up and developing as a person. The chances of developing an eating disorder may be influenced by a whole range of factors to do with the person herself, her family, their circumstances and the society in which they live. And, of course, there are all those unknown and unpredictable factors that we tend to call luck or the lack of it.

KEY POINTS

✓ A desire to lose weight is often the starting point for an eating disorder

✓ Family influences seem to play a part, but exactly what these are or how important they are is not known

✓ Most sufferers have low self-esteem

✓ Sufferers often have difficulty expressing their emotions

How eating disorders develop

Although we have discussed some of the possible factors that cause eating disorders, it still does not really explain exactly why they develop. The subject is a difficult one. There is much uncertainty. The following discussion attempts to give a view of one kind of explanation that weaves together some of the issues that were mentioned in the previous section. It is a way of looking at things but it is not to be taken as the last word or the whole truth about the nature of eating disorders. We are a long way from being able to claim to know that.

Eating disorders are not just about food and weight. They involve a complex web, or 'entanglement', of ideas linking weight and eating control with wider and more personal issues such as self-esteem and emotional control. People with eating disorders tend to think about and evaluate themselves in ways that involve weight and eating to an unusual and exaggerated degree. Although these topics are important to many people, for those with eating disorders it is the extent that is unusual and problematic. For instance, a woman with anorexia nervosa may feel that life would be almost intolerable if she was an average weight for her height and age. Strangely this may be the case even when she is willing to acknowledge that life was much better in the past when she was at a normal weight.

Many people say that anorexia nervosa is not really about weight or eating at all. Instead, they would say that it is about underlying problems of self-esteem and so on. And these underlying problems are seen as related to personal issues which are 'deeper' still.

There are problems with this way of thinking. Talking about these matters in terms of 'depth' implies that deeper issues are more basic and so more important. And because of this, issues of weight and eating can be dismissed as superficial. This can be avoided through the alternative way of thinking which sees the central issue as being the entanglement between ideas about weight and eating with ideas about wider personal issues. Indeed, in a sense the tangle is the eating disorder. However devastating the problems of self-esteem may be, if they are not somehow mixed up with issues of weight and eating, then the person does not have an eating disorder.

Once entangled with wider personal issues, weight and eating become more difficult to control. And these problems of control make it more difficult for the sufferer to manage the wider personal issues. This entanglement can lead to a vicious circle which is difficult to break. An important element in this vicious circle is the regulatory mechanisms which are normally involved in weight and eating control.

> *'Weight and eating control get entangled with wider personal issues'*

THE PROBLEM OF SLIMMING

Anyone who seeks to change his or her weight will run up against these natural regulatory mechanisms of the body. Nevertheless, most people approach the matter with high hopes and expectations based upon the widely held notion that losing weight and eating should be a simple matter. Most believe in the enticingly straightforward principle that if you eat too much your weight goes up, if you eat too little your weight will go down, and if you eat just the right amount your weight will be just what you want it to be. On this basis, it would seem that with just a bit of effort you can choose to be almost any weight, perhaps even any shape, that you want to be. I like to call this set of ideas 'the slimming philosophy'. It seems to be the ideology underlying the slimming industry.

However, this line of thinking has at least two drawbacks. First, it encourages a woman to feel that if she is not the weight she wishes to be (or feels that others would wish her to be) then it is not only her misfortune, it is also her fault. A woman who feels she is too fat is thus also likely to feel that she has not tried hard enough and is to blame for her state in a way that she would not do if it was her height with which she was dissatisfied.

The second drawback is that as a picture of weight and eating control the slimming philosophy is much too simple. It largely ignores the fact that our bodies have a marked tendency to maintain a certain stable weight. An alternative view of weight and eating control emphasises this stability. This alternative view suggests that the body tends to behave like a regulated system in respect of weight. Given the chance, each person's body tends to regulate itself naturally within a fairly narrow set range of weight particular for that individual. This personal set range may change over time as for instance in the commonplace phenomenon of 'middle-age spread'. Nevertheless for most people most of the time there seems to be a great deal of inherent stability of body weight. This means, of course, that body weight is not

simply a matter of personal preference as was suggested by the slimming philosophy. For better or worse the body as it were has a vote in the matter. The idea of regulation can be portrayed by the image of a spring which tends to come to rest always at more or less the same point.

Unfortunately, it does not follow that every person is satisfied with the particular weight around which his or her body tends to settle and regulate itself. Many people are dissatisfied and in our society this usually means that they wish to lose some weight. Indeed, many set out to do so. It is when people try to slim that the predictions of this alternative view involving regulation begin to differ markedly from those of the slimming philosophy. Most slimmers are surprised to encounter what might be called 'the dieter's dilemma'.

Regulating body weight

When a person sets out to slim it is because of some sense of dissatisfaction with herself. By definition slimmers are dissatisfied with their weight. However, this dissatisfaction is often more than a simple wish to change her body weight. She may feel that she wants to do something to sort herself out in general. Not uncommonly people go on a diet when things are not going well in other ways or when they are feeling badly about themselves. It may feel like a positive thing to do.

So typically, someone who resolves to go on a diet initially feels quite good about it. She feels better because of it and more in control of her life. However, after a while she will usually come to experience the downside of dieting. She may feel hungry and preoccupied with food, experience unwelcome impulses to eat and find herself to be more emotional and irritable than usual. The body's regulatory mechanisms are trying to fight against the dieter's attempts to push them out of kilter. The very things that previously promoted stability are pushing back and promoting a feeling of instability. The more the dieter pushes against them the more the forces push back. This is the 'dieter's dilemma'. The action of dieting has provoked a reaction by the body. Most dieters, if they are not succeeding in losing weight, will sooner or later give up, at least temporarily. And such 'failure' may be the key to avoiding the trap of eating disorders. People with eating disorders differ from most slimmers. They seem to persist with attempts to lose weight, even when they come up against the dieter's dilemma.

VICIOUS CIRCLES

Those who develop anorexia nervosa continue to try to lose weight to a point well beyond their original intention. Why is this? It seems likely that the potentially anorectic woman perseveres with slimming because she is afraid to give up. Either she has come to value the feeling of being in control or fears being out of control, or

both. She responds to her body's efforts to maintain a certain level of weight by attempting still tighter control. However, the regulatory forces (represented by the spring in the diagram on page 41) feel like a real threat to her sense of control. The more the spring is compressed the more it pushes back and comes to feel like a potential 'jack in the box'. Though it would be better for her to escape the trap by letting go, this increases the threat of failure and what feels like loss of control and she is too frightened to fail.

She has come to be caught up in the 'vicious circle of restraint'. She is not only trapped at a lower-than-intended weight. She is also in a position where controlling her eating and weight increasingly seems to be the only way of holding on to her insecure sense of well-being and control. She has anorexia nervosa.

The potentially bulimic woman may respond to the same developing vicious circle by giving in and bingeing. This is itself frightening. She then tries to resume tighter control and restraint, making another binge more likely.

She becomes caught up in the 'vicious circle of starving and bingeing'. Actions such as vomiting or laxative abuse tend to promote this vicious circle further. She has bulimia nervosa.

In both anorexia nervosa and bulimia nervosa, the issues of weight and eating control come to feel more and more crucial to the person's sense of well-being and self-esteem. The issues become more entangled with each other. The sufferer tries to make things better but in doing so makes them worse. She comes to feel that her attempts at self-improvement and self-control have ended up quite differently from what she had been aiming to achieve. She feels bad about herself but instead of letting go, she persists because not to do so seems even more risky. This persistence can lead to an even greater sense of failure and suffering. This is the 'vicious circle of entanglement'.

To recapitulate, this way of talking about eating disorders describes them as arising from a number of vicious circles which combine to entrap some people who persist in restraining their eating. The initial motivation for the restraint may reflect the individual's personal interpretation of the general social context which tends to value slimness and so on. Once started, the career of restraint may itself provoke effects which tend to lead it to continue. Mainly physiological mechanisms such as those portrayed by the spring may produce effects that are responded to in psychological ways. Likewise, the person's psychological response may lead to the physiological mechanisms being pushed further still.

Other changes in the body may take place as a result, including the 'switching off' of the adult hormonal patterns mentioned earlier, and these in turn may have psychological consequences. In the meantime, the sufferer will be feeling and behaving in a different way from usual and other people may be responding to her differently. For instance, she may come to be seen as a sick child rather than as a robust adolescent or as a quirky invalid, rather than a healthy adult. All sorts of con-sequences can come, tending to confirm the sufferer in her trapped position.

WHO IS MORE VULNERABLE?

The people most likely to be trapped by these vicious circles must in some way be especially vulnerable. However, we are not certain of what it is that makes some people more vulnerable than others.

It may in part be biological, as the genetic evidence suggests.

However, psychological factors are likely to be of crucial importance. It is likely that people struggling with certain emotional dilemmas may become more readily trapped. For instance, a person who feels she must keep tight control on her emotions, and/or is in a situation in which she is wary of rocking the boat, may find giving up slimming difficult. Anything that leads a woman to feel less secure and to value herself less may tip the balance towards things going wrong. (Both Heather and Susan in the stories given earlier could be thought of as being vulnerable in these ways.)

Also, some people seem to find any threat of instability and unpredictability especially difficult to cope with. They are often thought of as being perfectionist and obsessional. Although these personality traits have real advantages in some circumstances, they may make a person more vulnerable to eating disorders, perhaps especially to anorexia nervosa.

This section has outlined a way of discussing what eating disorders may be about. It may help to put together what may otherwise seem to be rather fragmented theories and ideas about the causes. However, I would like to emphasise that for the present there are more good questions than there are good answers about the nature of the eating disorders. Nevertheless, most people do recover from these somewhat mysterious disorders. The following chapters discuss what is involved in recovery and some of the methods that are used to help sufferers get better.

KEY POINTS

✓ The first step to an eating disorder is trying to reduce body weight by restraining eating

✓ Fear of failure and giving up may play a part in trapping people within eating disorders

✓ People with eating disorders come to have complicated attitudes towards weight, self-esteem and self-control

✓ Some people may be more vulnerable to eating disorders, for instance those who are obsessional and perfectionist

The road to recovery

Getting better from an eating disorder may be thought of as involving three tasks. These need to be tackled whether or not the sufferer recovers with treatment or, as sometimes happens, with little or no help from professionals. The tasks remain the same. It may be useful to outline these tasks before going on to discuss the treatments which may help the sufferer to address them.

Although the three tasks will be presented separately, they are closely linked. For someone trying to recover they will be all mixed up together. Furthermore, all three must be achieved if true recovery is to take place.

RESTORE A HEALTHY WEIGHT AND PATTERN OF EATING

The first task is for the sufferer to regain a sustainable and healthy body weight and pattern of eating. This involves the person giving up undue eating restraint and allowing her weight to find a level where it can naturally regulate itself. She must, as it were, rediscover a sense of natural control – an 'automatic pilot'. The sufferer needs to learn to trust the regulatory mechanisms of the body rather than fighting them all of the time. In practice, this involves eating regular meals of sufficient size. Carbohydrate may be especially important in restoring appropriate regulation of eating. Although easy to describe, this task may be very difficult for the sufferer to allow herself to do. The role of those helping someone to achieve this goal is to try to promote a sense of sufficient safety and security. This may involve trying to help the individual to feel that her eating will not run out of control once she starts. It does not involve simply pushing her to eat.

DISENTANGLE IDEAS OF WEIGHT FROM WIDER PERSONAL ISSUES

The second task is to disentangle ideas about weight and eating control from wider personal issues.

This is not only difficult to do but even difficult to think about in precise terms. Within our society some overlap and entanglement of such issues with self-esteem and so on is common. However, for women with eating disorders they become very mixed up. If she is to recover the sufferer must examine and then challenge the particular ideas that have come to determine so much of her behaviour. These could include ideas that to be thin is to be happy and successful or that if she is not vigilant her weight will go up and up in an uncontrolled fashion. She has to discover for herself the problems and limitations of such ideas. This task seems to involve thinking and perhaps talking. The person may also need to test out in practice the apparent truth or otherwise of some of these cherished ideas.

FACE PERSONAL ISSUES

Confronting particular personal issues which are relevant and problematic to each sufferer is crucial to recovery. And the problems that need to be tackled are likely to be as varied as the people who develop eating disorders.

If a woman with an eating disorder could magically accomplish the first and second tasks, she would still be confronted with all the problems and self-doubts that had previously been tangled up with weight and eating. Furthermore, months or years of such entanglement may have brought changes that are themselves problematic.

The third task then is to get life on the move again. This is often spoken of as getting life 'sorted out'. However, most people's lives are never truly sorted out, but involve a progression from one issue or problem to the next. Living entirely happily ever afterwards is for fairy tales. So a woman with an eating disorder must learn to move away from the behaviour in which she is trapped, going round and round in circles with the same problems. She must move on. In this respect it may be useful to consider once more the fictional accounts of the lives of Heather and Susan which were given earlier. Real lives are certainly no less complex.

> **'Life has to get on the move again'**

KEY POINTS: THE TASKS OF RECOVERY

✓ Restore a healthy and sustainable weight and pattern of eating

✓ Disentangle ideas about weight and eating from wider personal issues

✓ Begin to make progress with regard to these wider issues

Treatment for eating disorders

There is effective treatment for eating disorders. However, someone cannot receive appropriate treatment in a wholly passive manner and yet still recover, as might be the case with some physical illnesses. Struggling out of an eating disorder must be an active process on the part of the sufferer, even though others may help a great deal. Treatment should help the sufferer to define and to tackle the tasks of recovery herself.

Most people who find themselves with an eating disorder have very mixed feelings. On the one hand, they hate their present state; on the other, they fear changing it, because change may seem to threaten instability and a loss of control. The sufferer is caught up in a vicious circle and the easiest thing to do in a vicious circle is to stay within it.

Breaking out is always demanding. It demands courage and faith. Whatever approach is used, the overall aim of treatment must be to promote sufficient understanding, confidence and a sense of safety to enable the sufferer to change.

In many ways anorexia nervosa and bulimia nervosa are similar disorders, and the general tasks of recovery apply to both. However, there are differences in how these tasks are achieved. So, not surprisingly, the typical treatment advocated for the two disorders will differ although there are many elements in common.

It is important to emphasise that the following is only an outline of the current treatments. This does not mean that these treatments are perfect or will work for everyone. Some people recover without professional help, while a few fail to recover even though they have been through extensive treatment.

BULIMIA NERVOSA

The mainstay of treatment for bulimia nervosa is some sort of short-term psychotherapy, or 'talking treatment'. This involves the patient meeting with a therapist for a series of conversations, each typically lasting between half an hour and an hour. In this case short term means therapy involving between 12 and 24 sessions spread out over three to six months. There are often follow-up appointments at much longer intervals.

There are different kinds of psychotherapy. Probably the most successful in the treatment of bulimia nervosa is cognitive–behavioural psychotherapy, or CBT.

As the name suggests, CBT is focused upon both the problematic behaviours and the ideas (cognitions) that support them. The therapist works with the patient to reduce undesired behaviours, such as bingeing and vomiting, and to build up healthy alternatives such as eating more regularly. The patient is usually asked to keep a detailed diary so as to monitor the relevant

behaviours and the thoughts and feelings that seem to trigger them. As the problematic behaviours become less frequent the patient and her therapist can begin to see the wood for the trees. The ideas and beliefs that maintain the disorder become more evident and accessible to scrutiny and change.

If all goes well the last phase of the treatment is focused much more upon managing issues such as self-esteem than upon weight and eating control. CBT emphasises the need to find new ways of tackling present problems rather than speculating about why they developed. It recognises that what sustains a problem now may not be what caused it in the first place. Furthermore, it sees the present as more open to scrutiny and change.

Other types of psychotherapy can be used in the treatment of bulimia, although there is less evidence for their effectiveness. Some types of psychotherapy are very similar to CBT, whereas others are quite different. Some concentrate much more upon issues of current relationships. Still others, called psychodynamic therapies, are focused upon exploring links between the current symptoms and issues in the past, and tend to invoke the importance of unconscious mental processes. At present, we cannot be absolutely sure which kind of therapy is best in any one case.

However, some direct attention to the issue of eating does seem to be sensible and is supported by the evidence. In the terms outlined above, it makes sense that all three tasks should be addressed.

Hospital admission

Most treatment for bulimia nervosa takes place on an outpatient basis. However, some people may benefit from hospital admission. This may be especially useful if bulimia is only one of several problems that feel

TREATMENT FOR BULIMIA NERVOSA

- Short-term psychotherapy, mainly cognitive–behavioural psychotherapy
- Other types of psychotherapy
- Hospital admission is occasionally useful
- Treatment with antidepressant drugs may sometimes be helpful

out of control. For instance, the woman may be drinking excessively, taking drugs, shoplifting or experiencing impulses to harm herself. This is sometimes called multi-impulsive bulimia.

Special inpatient programmes exist for bulimia in general and such complicated bulimia in particular. These can be helpful but their advantages over simpler treatments have not yet been clearly proven.

The same goes for other special regimes that are built around the so-called Twelve Step programmes. These are based on ideas similar to those used in Alcoholics Anonymous and some approaches to drug dependence. How applicable these are to eating disorders is a matter of debate.

Dealing with depression

In many cases bulimia nervosa may be accompanied by clinical depression, and antidepressant drug therapy may be very useful. Antidepressants are not 'pep pills' and are not addictive. They can help when someone has symptoms of depression, such as low spirits, poor sleep and reduced vitality. It is possible that some antidepressant drugs also have a direct effect upon the bulimic symptoms. This seems to be a modest effect, however, and in most cases medication alone is not adequate treatment for bulimia nervosa.

When additional help is needed

Sometimes the sufferer makes great progress in separating weight and eating from wider issues. However, she may find that these issues are still causing problems or are associated with other kinds of distress or problematic ways of coping. For instance, she may be clinically depressed or drinking excessively. If so, therapy may need to be adapted and often extended.

Hospital admission may be recommended to help her cope with crises or to help gain some initial sense of control. Even when there are no major complications, some people decide that they want more wide-ranging psychotherapy to explore their feelings after they have overcome the particular disorder of bulimia nervosa.

Sometimes people need a good deal more than short-term psychotherapy. Others recover using a self-help approach in which they follow advice given to them in written form with or without some face-to-face sessions with a therapist. And it must be remembered that some people recover without any outside help at all.

ANOREXIA NERVOSA

The treatment of anorexia nervosa is usually more prolonged than that of bulimia nervosa. It may take months and years rather than weeks and months. This is partly because the

TREATMENT FOR ANOREXIA NERVOSA

- Psychotherapy:
  cognitive–behavioural psychotherapy
  psychodynamic therapy
- Hospital admission
- Family therapy, especially for younger sufferers
- Self-help organisations can complement professional help

person with anorexia nervosa has the initial task of restoring her weight and then learning to maintain it once restored. Furthermore, once an individual has developed full-blown anorexia nervosa the degree of entanglement is usually much more profound although there are exceptions to this rule.

For the person trying to escape from anorexia nervosa the first of the three tasks of recovery – regaining lost weight – tends to loom large. It also 'looms large' for those around her. The emaciation of those with severe anorexia nervosa is so pressingly evident that it may come to dominate the picture and sometimes it is appropriate that it should do so. However, the second and third tasks are every bit as important in the long run. Any treatment programme that neglects them is unlikely to be effective.

Help from psychotherapy
Most treatment for anorexia nervosa can take place on an outpatient basis. As with bulimia nervosa, the core treatment should involve some kind of psychotherapy which enables the patient to feel safe enough to change. Cognitive–behavioural techniques may be used or more exploratory styles of a psychodynamic kind.

Often some kind of monitoring of weight and eating is incorporated into the therapy. The therapist or a colleague may need to advise the sufferer on how to change her eating habits. This is not because the task is complex or difficult, but because the patient needs to feel safe when performing the simple act of eating and choosing what to eat. She has to borrow confidence from someone whom she can trust.

The important thing is that the whole process helps the individual feel confident enough to let go of some of the exaggerated control that she is exerting upon herself. This control is both dietary and psychological, so the process of psychological change depends in part on physical change. Sometimes the task of gaining weight proves too difficult, and the patient remains stuck in her behaviour or even deteriorates. A more intensive treatment situation may be required, and hospital admission needs to be considered.

When hospital treatment is needed

Admission to hospital can be frightening. Ideally the patient needs to decide for herself that it is the way forward. The best reason for admission is that the patient herself wants to change but cannot do so except with constant, round-the-clock support. Again the aim should be to promote a sense of confidence, trust and safety.

If the sufferer feels that she is being bundled into hospital, for instance because her health is endangered, she may feel even more out of control. In these situations people are liable to panic. If it is the patient who is panicking, she may make the right decision and go into hospital but often her resolve will waver before long. If it is the family or the doctors who are feeling that there is no choice but hospital treatment, a battle may ensue.

Such battles between a patient with an eating disorder and those who are trying to help her are

sometimes difficult to avoid. However, they usually make matters worse. The patient may find initially that she had mixed feelings about going into hospital, but pressure from others frees her whole-heartedly to oppose them. It is easier to battle with others than it is to have a battle raging within oneself.

Very occasionally compulsory admission under a provision of the Mental Health Act may be sought on the justification that inpatient treatment is required to save the patient from serious deterioration of health or even death. However, such situations are best avoided if at all possible. Those involved with the sufferer need to try to cherish and work with the more positive aspects of her feelings.

Admission to hospital should provide a good setting for tackling all three of the tasks of recovery. Probably the best chance of this happening is if the sufferer is admitted to a unit specialising in the treatment of severe anorexia nervosa. Most specialist inpatient services are located in psychiatric hospitals or in the psychiatric units of general hospitals. Unfortunately there are rather few of these, and there may often be a difficult choice between admission to such a specialist service far away or to a more local but less specialised psychiatric or medical unit.

> **'The sufferer has to feel safe enough to eat'**

Hospital treatment is usually geared towards encouraging the patient to gain weight. Often a target weight is set and the person aims to reach and then maintain this weight. In most cases the patient achieves this by eating substantial, healthy meals. Special food supplements may be useful, but techniques such as tube feeding are hardly ever justifiable.

Most inpatient treatment regimes have their own rules and regulations about eating. Many of these are essentially arbitrary but make the whole experience more predictable, and predictability can bring a sense of safety. It helps the patient feel that she will be prevented from overeating once she starts. The details of the regime, the confidence of the nursing staff and the general emotional setting can all help her to feel safe enough to eat.

The more specific, psychotherapeutic treatment needs to continue alongside the weight restoration regime and indeed should continue long after weight is regained. As the patient gains weight she will need an opportunity to talk openly about her thoughts and emotions. Furthermore, restoring body weight only marks the start of another phase of recovery rather than its completion. In fact, restoring weight may often seem to be the easiest part of recovery to both the patient and those who are trying to help her.

The role of the family

For younger patients with anorexia nervosa who are still living with their parent or parents, family therapy of some kind is often thought to be useful. This may be addressed to all three of the tasks of recovery. For instance, the family may be asked to take responsibility for feeding their child. More often, family therapy involves trying to understand and change the emotional issues that have become entangled with weight and eating.

Where to get help

A variety of different people and services offers treatment for eating disorders. The family doctor (GP) will be the usual first contact for someone who is seeking help. Sometimes the GP is able to provide all that is required, but often referral will be made to a more specialist service.

In some parts of the country there are services devoted to the assessment and treatment of eating disorders. Some of these will be able to deal with the full range of eating disorders of every type and severity. Others are suitable only for the less severe.

An important issue is the extent to which the person or service is able to provide assessment, monitoring and intervention for both the psychological and the physical aspects of the disorders. A general physician may feel comfortable treating the physical problems but less so with the

psychological ones. A psychotherapist may have the reverse problem. What is important is that, somehow, all the necessary aspects are sufficiently addressed.

Usually within the NHS, help for eating disorders is offered within the mental health services which tend to be organised into multidisciplinary teams. In addition to the medically qualified psychiatrist, nurses, clinical psychologists, occupational therapists and social workers will be involved. This pooling of available skills often helps, although the key contact may still be with just one person. Patients who are in their mid-teens or younger would normally be offered help within Child Psychiatric Services.

Self-help organisations

Another important resource is the self-help groups which are widely available throughout the country. These can provide useful information, advice and support for both sufferers and their families. Most would claim to be a complement rather than an alternative to professional help. Many are organised by the Eating Disorders Association, the address of which is given at the end of this book (see page 66).

KEY POINTS

✓ Psychotherapy is often the first line of treatment for eating disorders

✓ Most treatment can take place on an outpatient basis

✓ Antidepressant drugs may help ease depression

✓ Hospital treatment is more common in anorexia nervosa

✓ Some hospitals have specialist units dealing with the treatment of eating disorders

Advice for family and friends

F amily and friends often worry that someone they care about may have an eating disorder. It may be that the friend or relative has lost a considerable amount of weight or worries about her weight constantly. She may appear overly interested in food or furtive about her eating habits.

The descriptions of anorexia nervosa and bulimia nervosa included earlier in this book contain lists of particular signs and symptoms of the illnesses. Some of these will be obvious, such as a very low weight, whereas others may be

IS IT AN EATING DISORDER?

- Most people with an eating disorder are unhappy. They may hide this beneath a brittle cheerfulness, but people who know them may not be misled.

- Most people with an eating disorder are touchy about their weight. It becomes something that is vitally important to them, and they seem to have got the whole thing out of proportion.

- Most people with an eating disorder try to eat very little. Sometimes they will try to mislead those around them into thinking that they are eating more than they are.

- Many people with an eating disorder are vomiting or taking laxatives. They will do this in secret, but going off to the lavatory after every meal and returning looking flustered should arouse suspicion.

- Many people with an eating disorder become very interested in cooking for others or telling them what they should and should not eat. The whole topic of weight and eating becomes highly charged. The same may be true of exercise.

- Many people with an eating disorder wear baggy clothes and take other steps to hide their figures.

- Most people with an eating disorder seem changed from their usual selves.

entirely hidden, for instance secret binges or vomiting.

You may have noticed other signs that are much less specific. Some of these are listed in the box. Remember, though, that none of these features is present just in eating disorders. The presence of one or even all of them is not enough to determine that someone definitely has an eating disorder. However, if some of these are clearly present and causing you concern, then it may be time to think about sharing your concerns with the person involved.

BROACHING THE SUBJECT
There is no way to be sure that someone has an eating disorder

unless the person confides her thoughts and worries. To turn a suspicion into something more definite, it is necessary to talk. But do not jump to conclusions, and do not panic.

Choosing the right moment to bring up the subject is important. However, having chosen the moment you should share your worries in a direct manner. This is better than beating about the bush. It may be a hot topic but it needs to be approached with a cool head and a warm manner. Pushing too hard for answers may make the patient more defensive.

Parents can sometimes feel that home has become a battleground, with food as a powerful weapon. They can feel guilty and responsible for what is happening to their child. This is not a useful starting point for tackling the problems of eating disorders.

Someone with an eating disorder may be relieved to share her trouble, although she may not. Eating disorders are often a private form of suffering, and that person may be wary of talking for all sorts of reasons. Eating disorders in general and anorexia nervosa in particular may give the person a tenuous but valued sense of personal control. Letting someone know all about it may seem to threaten this control in a frightening way.

The very person who is worried may be involved in some of the issues that are caught up in the problem. The sufferer might find it difficult to broach the topic and be open about her feelings; open discussion of everything is not, however, necessary.

To get things started, the sufferer must come to feel safe enough to take the risk of confiding some of her fears. Often the best person to hear the full story may be someone once removed from the sufferer's immediate family. This may be a teacher, friend or some other trusted person. If she has an eating disorder, the family doctor would be an appropriate first port of call in the search for help.

> '*Most people with an eating disorder seem changed from their usual selves*'

PUTTING UP WALLS
The person with the condition may not admit the problem, or she may not want help even if she will acknowledge that she has a

problem. The whole thing may be too fraught with fears and mixed feelings. One way of coping with mixed feelings is to get into an argument, where both parties find themselves expressing their views in more and more extreme terms. This usually gets nowhere.

In situations like these, it is usually best to back off and let everyone cool down rather than allow it to develop into a fight. Things are rarely so extreme that a few days will make matters worse. Someone cannot be forced to overcome fears and to trust another person. Trying too hard to make this happen cannot help.

It may be difficult for the worried parent, partner or friend to give space to the person about whom they are worried. Going behind that person's back to seek help is not a good idea. It may be helpful to talk to a relevant professional, such as the family doctor, about their own dilemma. Likewise, self-help organisations such as the Eating Disorders Association offer valuable support and advice to relatives and friends of people with eating disorders.

BEING IN CONTROL

Everyone, even children to a degree, has the right to be in control of their own lives. Fears about control seem to be central to eating disorders.

It is therefore not surprising that real conflicts can arise when a fearful sufferer and a worried parent or friend confront the issue of what to do next. Personal autonomy includes the possibility of making one's own mistakes.

In most circumstances the sufferer eventually comes to feel that more is to be lost by staying where she is than by risking change. She may have to come to this decision in her own time. Only in very extreme circumstances, where the person's life is in danger, is it justifiable to coerce someone into any form of treatment. And such circumstances are rare.

Perhaps it is best to recall the overall message of this book. Eating disorders are a serious matter, but they are not a reason to panic.

KEY POINTS

✓ Eating disorders can affect everyone around the sufferer, not just the person herself

✓ Choose the right time to bring up the subject

✓ If the sufferer does not want to discuss it, back off and try again at another time

✓ Avoid confrontations about her condition and about food

✓ Eating disorders are about control. Allow the person to make decisions for herself

✓ Ask for professional advice and help. But remember, it is rarely appropriate to force a person to accept treatment

What is the outlook?

Developing an eating disorder need not be a lifetime sentence. For some sufferers, it is a brief episode which lasts just a few months or even weeks. They then move on without many lasting or harmful effects. They tend not to seek help and do not appear in medical accounts of the disorders. Yet they certainly exist. What makes them so fortunate is not at all clear.

For a very few others, eating disorders prove fatal. Some studies have indicated that as many as 10 or even 20 per cent of people with anorexia nervosa die of the disorder. These figures are taken from follow-up studies of some of the very severe cases first seen many years ago. They are a gross overestimate of the death rate from eating disorders.

However, people do die from both anorexia nervosa and bulimia nervosa, either through the physical effects of the disorders or through suicide. It is difficult to be certain of the exact size of the problem. Perhaps one sufferer in 100 will die from the disorders. And having one of these disorders greatly increases the risk of a young woman dying prematurely.

In between these two extremes are most of those who suffer, for whom an eating disorder is an unpleasant and limiting fact of life. It can continue for months or, more usually, for years. A proportion of people with anorexia nervosa, perhaps one in 10, develop a truly

> **'Developing an eating disorder need not be a lifetime sentence'**

chronic illness which lasts for many years and from which some may never recover. This is probably also true of bulimia nervosa although the evidence is not so clear.

Some people in this position struggle to lead their lives as normally as they can. They are limited by their illness and may be dominated by it but somehow they get by. Others are so overwhelmed by their condition that it affects all aspects of their lives. Nevertheless, people can and do make progress or even recover completely even after many years. There is always a chance of getting better.

KEY POINTS

✓ Most sufferers of eating disorders make a full recovery

✓ Some recover on their own, without any outside help or treatment

✓ Eating disorders can be fatal

✓ Most people with the condition have an eating disorder for months or even years

Conclusion

Eating disorders must be taken seriously. A person may fall into the trap of an eating disorder without any intention of doing so. She may start out feeling that controlling her weight and eating is a way of getting her life together. But she ends up trapped in a vicious circle from which she cannot easily escape.

Once established, anorexia nervosa or bulimia nervosa can seriously affect a person's life. Sometimes the outcome is a truly chronic illness or even, rarely, death. However, even when this is not the case the disorders put a blight upon important and potentially enjoyable years.

Yet if these disorders are taken seriously by the sufferer and by those who wish to help her, she can escape. A number of effective treatments exist which can offer a good chance of recovery. The experience of being ill and trying to recover can be upsetting and frightening. Getting better is demanding and unfortunately the required courage cannot simply be prescribed, as can a medicine. The sufferer cannot expect that escaping from a vicious circle will be easy. What she should be able to expect is that those around her should have some understanding of her dilemma and that they take her and her problem seriously.

Panic is neither justified nor helpful. It simply leads the sufferer to cling even more tightly to her old ideas and ways of coping. Panic in those around her can push the sufferer further into her corner.

The great majority of people with either one of the eating disorders do recover. Perhaps all sufferers could do so, given appropriate support and treatment. No one need be without hope of recovery. Sooner or later an eating disorder can become a nightmare that is truly past.

Useful information

USEFUL ORGANISATIONS

Benefits Enquiry Line
Tel: 0800 882200
Website: www.dwp.gov.uk
Minicom: 0800 243355
N. Ireland: 0800 220674

Government agency giving information and advice on sickness and
disability benefits for people with
disabilities and their carers.

Eating Disorders Association
1st Floor, Wensum House
103 Prince of Wales Road
Norwich, Norfolk NR1 1DW
Tel: 0870 770 3256
Fax: 01603 664 915
Helpline: 0845 634 1414
(8.30am–8.30pm; Sat 1–4.30pm)
Textphone: 01603 753 322 (weekdays)
Youthline: 0845 634 7650
Email: info@edauk.com
Website: www.edauk.com

Offers information, help and support to anyone affected by eating
disorders – anorexia and bulimia
nervosa. Has local self-help groups.

First Steps to Freedom
1 Taylor Close
Kenilworth
Warwick CV8 2LW
Tel: 01926 864473
Fax: 01926 864473
Helpline: 0845 120 2916 (10am–10pm)
Email: first.steps@btconnect.com
Website: www.first-steps.org

Offers confidential helpline 365
days a year for sufferers of phobias,
anxiety, panic attacks and eating
disorders. Also gives practical
advice on overcoming symptoms of
withdrawal from tranquillisers.
Audio tapes and booklets available.

National Institute for Clinical Excellence (NICE)
MidCity Place
71 High Holborn
London WC1V 6NA
Tel: 020 7067 5800
Fax: 020 7067 5801
Email: nice@nice.nhs.uk
Website: www.nice.org.uk

Provides guidance on treatments and care for people using the NHS in England and Wales. Patient information leaflets are available for each piece of guidance issued.

Overeaters Anonymous
PO Box 32941
London SW20 8FW
National Helpline: 07000 784985
Email: info@oa.org
Website: www.oagb.org.uk/

A fellowship of men and women offering mutual support in recovering from a variety of compulsive eating disorders. Publishes information and offers mentoring system from people who have personal experience of eating disorders.

SUGGESTED FURTHER READING
The following books may give useful further information:

Helping People with Eating Disorders by R.L. Palmer, Wiley. 2000.

A longer description of eating disorders by the present author.

Anorexia Nervosa: A Guide for Sufferers and Their Families by R.L. Palmer. Penguin Books, 1989.

A longer description of anorexia nervosa by the present author.

Bulimia Nervosa: A Guide to Recovery by P.J. Cooper. Robinson Publishing, 1995.

Getting Better Bit(e) by Bit(e). A Survival Kit for Sufferers of Bulimia Nervosa and Binge Eating Disorders by U. Schmidt & J. Treasure. Lawrence Erlbaum, 1994.

Overcoming Binge Eating by C. Fairburn. Guilford Press, 1995.

Each of the last three books sets out to provide both increased understanding and a basic self-help programme for use by the reader. All three have been demonstrated to be useful in practice.

The following books are recommended by the Eating Disorders Association:

Anorexia Nervosa: A Guide to Recovery by L. Hall & M. Ostroff. Gurze Design & Books, 1998.

Talking about Anorexia by M. Monro. Sheldon, 1996.

Dealing with Eating Disorders by K. Haycock. Wayland, 1994.

Anorexia Nervosa and The Wish to Change by A. Crisp, N. Joughin, C. Halek & C. Bowyer. Lawrence Erlbaum, 1989.

Coping with Bulimia by B. French, Thorsons. 1994.

I Looked in the Mirror and Screamed by L. Ojeda. Piccadilly, 1993.

Males with Eating Disorders, edited by A.E. Andersen. Brunner/Mazel, 1990.

Eating Disorders and Obesity: A Comprehensive Handbook, 2nd edn, edited by C. Fairburn & K. Brownell. Guilford Press, 2001.

Eating Disorders: Anorexia nervosa, bulimia nervosa and related eating disorders. Understanding NICE guidance: a guide for people with eating disorders, their advocates and carers and the public. NICE, 2004.

THE INTERNET AS A SOURCE OF FURTHER INFORMATION

After reading this book, you may feel that you would like further information on the subject. One source is the internet and there are a great many websites with useful information about medical disorders, related charities and support groups. Some websites, however, have unhelpful and inaccurate information. Many are sponsored by commercial organisations or raise revenue by advertising, but nevertheless aim to provide impartial and trustworthy health information. Others may be reputable but you should be aware that they may be biased in their recommendations. Remember that treatment advertised on international websites may not be available in the UK.

Unless you know the address of the specific website that you want to visit (for example, familydoctor.co.uk), you may find the following guidelines helpful when searching the internet.

There are several different sorts of websites that you can use to look for information, the main ones being search engines, directories and portals.

Search engines and directories

There are many search engines and directories that all use different algorithms (procedures for computation) to return different results when you do a search. Search engines use computer programs called spiders, which crawl the web on a daily basis to search individual pages within a site and then queue them ready for listing in their database.

Directories, however, consider a site as a whole and use the description and information that was provided with the site when it was submitted to the directory to decide whether a site matches the searcher's needs. For both there is little or no selection in terms of quality of information, although engines and directories do try to impose rules about decency and content. Popular search engines in the UK include:

google.co.uk
aol.co.uk
msn.co.uk
lycos.co.uk
hotbot.co.uk
overture.com
ask.co.uk
espotting.com
looksmart.co.uk
alltheweb.com
uk.altavista.com

The two biggest directories are:

yahoo.com
dmoz.org

Portals

Portals are doorways to the internet that provide links to useful sites, news and other services, and may also provide search engine services (such as msn.co.uk). Many portals charge for putting their clients' sites high up in your list of search results. The quality of the websites listed depends on the selection criteria used in compiling the portal, although portals focused on a specific group, such as medical information portals, may have more rigorous inclusion criteria than other searchable websites. Examples of medical portals can be found at:

nhsdirect.nhs.uk
patient.co.uk

Links to many British medical charities will be found at the Association of Medical Research Charities (www.amrc.org.uk) and Charity Choice (www.charitychoice. co.uk).

Search phrases

Be specific when entering a search phrase. Searching for information on 'cancer' could give astrological information as well as medical: 'lung cancer' would be a better choice. Either use the engine's advanced search feature and ask for the exact phrase, or put the phrase in quotes – 'lung cancer' – as this will link the words. Adding 'uk' to your search phrase will bring up mainly British websites, so a good search would be 'lung cancer' uk (don't include uk within the quotes).

Always remember that the internet is international and unregulated. Although it holds a wealth of invaluable information, individual websites may be biased, out of date or just plain wrong. Family Doctor Publications accepts no responsibility for the content of links published in their series.

Index